# THE
# Sun
## OUR VERY OWN STAR

An Earlybird Book
## by Jeanne Bendick

Illustrated by Mike Roffe

## THE MILLBROOK PRESS INC.
### BROOKFIELD, CONNECTICUT

Cataloging-in-Publication Data

Bendick, Jeanne
The sun, our very own star.
Brookfield, CT, Millbrook Press, 1991.
32 p.; ill.: (Early Bird)
Includes index
ISBN 1-878841-02-5   523.7   BEN
1. Sun   2. Solar system   3. Stars.

Published by The Millbrook Press Inc, 2 Old New Milford Road, Brookfield,
Connecticut 06804, USA

Produced by Eagle Books Limited, Vigilant House, 120 Wilton Road,
London SW1V 1JZ, England

# Contents

# The Sun

What lights the day?
What heats the Earth?
What makes plants grow?

What keeps the planets in their places?
It's a certain star.
It's the Sun.

Did you know that the Sun is a star?

Our Sun isn't all that special in the universe. It's an ordinary, middle-sized yellow star. There are 100 billion other stars like it in our neighborhood in space, the **Milky Way Galaxy.**

We are here